Please Understand

Marcy L. Peake

THE CENTER FOR CULTURAL AGILITY
KALAMAZOO, MICHIGAN 49019

ISBN # 978-0-692-83081-9
Printed in the United States of America

Second Printing

For information or to order additional books, please contact:

Marcy L. Peake
P.O. Box 20004
Kalamazoo, Michigan, 49019
U.S.A.

Or visit our website for online ordering at: *www.thecenterforculturalagility.com*

Dedication

To my mom and dad, Crispy Toast and Jelly;
without you, I would not be me.

To my family for contributing to my value system and sense of
defending those most in need of protection.

To my husband for always keeping it real; all day, every day.

To the educators, therapists, and youth development
professionals who already understand.

And graciously, to my young people and their families for
trusting me with your hearts, souls, insecurities, and dreams.
This is for you, because of you...

Please
Understand...

That the walk to my bus is
dangerous and scary.
But I make it every day to see you
and learn.

Please
Understand...

That I do not always have the words to tell you what is wrong. But I can break and throw things to communicate my feelings.

Please
Understand...

That yes, I do look different
from you.
But notice our differences
and don't place judgement on them.

Please
Understand...

That I get more anxious when you yell and become demanding. Usually yelling and anger lead to someone getting hurt at my house.

Please
Understand...

That I might want to leave my shoes on and not participate. We don't have a washer or dryer and my socks are dirty.

Please Understand...

That yes, I stole a banana.
Even bananas have value when you
don't have anything.

Please
Understand...

That I don't look forward to holidays or summer vacation. These are not happy or safe times for me.

Please
Understand...

That I don't know how to make
and keep friends.
We have moved 4 times this year
and I have a hard enough time
remembering your name and what I
have to do to keep you liking me.

Please
Understand...

That yes, I do "act grown."
I have to at home because the
grown-ups don't.

Please
Understand...

That I know exactly who I am talking about when I say, "my cousin's sister's boyfriend's uncle." Until a name is made up for my relationship to this person, that's what I have to call them.

Please
Understand...

That I might continue to ask for more cereal or another hotdog. I won't get to eat again until I come back to school tomorrow.

Please
Understand...

That I do talk loud and blurt out. But when there are many voices yelling in my house, I have to in order to be heard.

Please
Understand...

That I do not complete my assignments sometimes.
It is not because I don't want to, it is because I can't.

Please
Understand...

That I am telling you the truth
when I say, "I don't know" when you
ask, "what would your parents say?"
I don't have parents.

Please
Understand...

That I shut down sometimes.
But it is not because of you, my
mind and body need a break.

Please

Understand...

That no one has ever shown me that there is a time and place for everything.
So I do what I want, when I want.

Please
Understand...

That I can't have my photo in the school paper.
My family ran from a dangerous and mean person.

Please
Understand...

That the grown-ups in my house did
not sign my permission slip.
They can't read.

Please
Understand...

A bath, clean pajamas, and a
bedtime story are other untruths
in my world.
We don't have running water,
pajamas, or beds.

Please
Understand...

That my body moves and sounds
come out without warning.
I was born addicted to alcohol and
crack.

Please
Understand...

That being late means
nothing to me.
I think it is possible for
the clock to say 2:75 o'clock.

Please
Understand...

That I don't know or can't say what I will be when I grow up.
A dealer, hustler, or someone who sells their kids or food stamps for drugs would not be acceptable answers.

Please
Understand...

That I need to back away when you touch me or come close.
It makes me uncomfortable because other adults have touched me and I have to keep it a secret.

Please
Understand...

That when I say,
"I don't want to live anymore"
what I really mean is,
that I don't want to live the life I
have anymore.

Please
Understand...

That I need you to be kind to me.
I count on you to be kind to me.

Please
Understand...

That although I am responsible for my behavior, I am not responsible for what I have been taught.
So please take the time to be kind to me.

I will share my life with you if only you will allow yourself to see my life through my eyes.
Once you do that, I will feel accepted by you and will no longer be embarrassed or feel judged by you.

I will come to you to help me and you will not only be able to teach me new things but un-teach me some of the other things.

Here are some things I thought might help you, help me:

If I walk through your door and look grumpy:

1. Give me space, but please don't ignore me. Let me know you noticed I am troubled about something and you will be willing to listen when I can talk.

2. Ask me if I need breakfast. This allows me dignity to say a simple "yes" without having to answer in front of everyone that I do not get food at home.

3. In private, find out if I got hurt or watched someone or something I care about be hurt. I have been taught to guard these secrets but once I feel that I can trust you and you care enough to help, I will tell you.

4. Don't take my moods personally. It's not about you, it's about me. Nothing in my life is within my control except my moods and my face.

When I hesitate to answer you:

1. Stop and think why I might be reluctant; I might not know the answer, I might not be able to say the answer, or I might be too ashamed to answer. If you think of these three reasons and who else is around, why I am not answering will probably make sense and not make you angry.

2. Don't decide that I am being defiant and make things worse. Nothing you say or do to me in anger or frustration really matters, I hear worse and have worse done to me at home by the people who are supposed to love me the most. This will only push me further away from you.

3. A lot of times, I am afraid to answer grown-ups. At home when I answer wrong, I get hit which not only hurts my body but my soul too.

4. Don't use my name harshly against me. It's the only thing I have that is mine. Please don't turn that into something I dread hearing.

If I refuse to participate:

1. I probably lack confidence. I am used to being told I can't do anything right so I have stopped trying.

2. I might not have what I need to participate. Homework requires certain things, I am too embarrassed to tell you that we don't have lights and I can't see in the house past dark. Try to find a way for me to be successful while I am at school with the supplies I need.

3. Take me aside and ask me respectfully why. If you embarrass me, I have learned that it is easier to "act-out" in front of my classmates and get sent out of class than be teased by them for why I can't do something.

4. Find alternate ways that I can participate or make up the work so I still have to do what everyone else is expected to do, but that I have what I need so I am able to do what everyone else is expected to do.